MONSTER MADNESS!

More Than 600 Frightfully Funny Jokes, Riddles & Puns

John Briggs

STERLING CHILDREN'S BOOKS
New York

To Kara, for liking Halloween
more than anyone I know
—J.B.

STERLING CHILDREN'S BOOKS
New York

An Imprint of Sterling Publishing Co., Inc.
1166 Avenue of the Americas
New York, NY 10036

STERLING CHILDREN'S BOOKS and the distinctive Sterling Children's
Books logo are registered trademarks of Sterling Publishing Co., Inc.

ISBN 978-1-4549-3057-0

Distributed in Canada by Sterling Publishing Co., Inc.
c/o Canadian Manda Group, 664 Annette Street
Toronto, Ontario M6S 2C8, Canada
Distributed in the United Kingdom by GMC Distribution Services
Castle Place, 166 High Street, Lewes, East Sussex BN7 1XU, England
Distributed in Australia by NewSouth Books
University of New South Wales, Sydney, NSW 2052, Australia

For information about custom editions, special sales, and premium
and corporate purchases, please contact Sterling Special Sales at
800-805-5489 or specialsales@sterlingpublishing.com.

Manufactured in Canada

Lot #:
2 4 6 8 10 9 7 5 3 1

08/19

sterlingpublishing.com

Cover design and illustration by Julie Robine
Interior design by Julie Robine

For Photo/Image credits, see page 96

Contents

THE FUN DEAD

What do you call zombies who follow you?
The Stalking Dead.

Why did the zombie chase his cousin?
She had the brains in the family.

How do you know when a zombie is spoiled?
He's rotten to the corpse.

Why don't zombies talk back?
Because they never get fresh.

HEHE

What do you never take around a zombie?
A deep breath.

When are zombies made?
During the graveyard shift.

When do zombies party?
In the dead of night.

HA HA HA HA HA HA HA HA
HA HA HA HA HA HA HA HA

What do you call it when a zombie invites friends to stay at his graveyard?

A sleep under.

- -

Where do zombies cool off in the summer?

A drool party.

LOL

- -

How does a zombie cross a pool?

Dead man's float.

- -

Why do zombies read the obituaries?

To find new friends.

- -

Why do zombies have tiny headstones?

Because a little slab will do ya.

- -

How do you keep zombies in the ground?

Put them in a *cement*ery.

- -

Why does a zombie carry a thick, black pen?

It's her grave marker.

- -

Why did the magician levitate a zombie?

He was raising the dead.

- -

HAHAHA HA HA

Where do zombies go on vacation?

The Dead Sea.

What kind of hair does a zombie have?

Deadlocks.

Why couldn't the zombie turn on his flashlight?

His batteries were dead, too.

How do zombies get so much energy?

Brain power.

What type of shoes do zombies wear?

*Ghoul*ashes.

Why can't zombies make a decision?

They drag their feet.

How do you know when a zombie is serious?

She has a grave face.

What do you call a zombie sharpshooter?

Deadeye.

Why do zombies sound like frogs?

They croaked.

What makes a zombie fall in a cemetery?

Graveity.

- -

What's the worst punishment a judge can give a zombie?

The undeath sentence.

- -

Where does a zombie build his house?

On a dead-end street.

- -

Where do zombies get their mail?

The dead letter office.

- -

What do you call a plane full of zombies?

Flight of the Living Dead.

- -

What do zombies say before starting a car?

"Let her R.I.P.!"

- -

Why don't you buy anything from a zombie?

It costs an arm and a leg.

- -

How did the zombie break a tooth?

Bit into a kidney stone.

- -

What's a zombie's favorite game?

Got Your Nose.

What does a zombie say when a person acts annoyed?

"Who's gnawing you?"

Which insects act like drones?

Zombees.

How does a zombie get into a fancy party?

Worms his way in.

What do zombies call Albert Einstein?

Brain food.

What do you call a zombie with a day job?

Dad.

Knock-knock!

Who's there?

Debugs

Debugs who?

Debugs on de zombies are disgusting.

FANGTASTIC JOKES

What did the vampire say when his fangs grew in?

"This bites!"

Why did the vampire go to a cheap dentist?

He wanted more fang for his buck.

What should you never do when defending a vampire?

Stick your neck out.

What happened when the vampire sneezed?

She got a bloody nose.

What do you call a vampire with a good sense of smell?

Nose Feratu.

LOL

What do vampires do at night?

Fang out.

What do bored vampires do?

Fang around.

Why can't you trust a vampire's hair?

It's too slick.

How do vampires get clean?

They take a blood bath.

Where do vampires get clean?

In a *bat*tub.

Where do vampires buy clothes?

Pantsylvania.

What do you call a vampire with big hair
and makeup?

A glampire.

Why doesn't Dracula gamble?

He doesn't like the stakes.

Why are vampires so serious about stakes?

They take them to heart.

Who is a vampire's favorite person?

A blood donor.

What's the nicest thing you can say to a vampire?

"Bite me!"

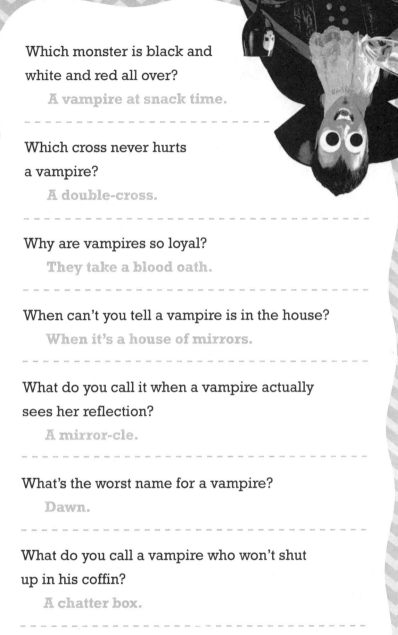

Which monster is black and white and red all over?

A vampire at snack time.

Which cross never hurts a vampire?

A double-cross.

Why are vampires so loyal?

They take a blood oath.

When can't you tell a vampire is in the house?

When it's a house of mirrors.

What do you call it when a vampire actually sees her reflection?

A mirror-cle.

What's the worst name for a vampire?

Dawn.

What do you call a vampire who won't shut up in his coffin?

A chatter box.

What do you call a vampire's siblings?

Blood brothers.

What did Dracula say when he found out his wife had O Negative blood?

"You're my type."

What does Dracula say to unhappy people?

"Great. B Negative."

Why did the vampire hunter carry garlic?

It goes well with *stake*.

What did the stupid vampire say when the judge said, "Order in the court!"

"I'll take two more victims."

What does a vampire do in art school?

A blood draw.

What does a vampire do after she makes her bed?

Closes the coffin lid.

What do you say when a vampire gets furious?

"He blew a casket."

Why does Dracula slick down his hair when he wakes up?

He has coffin head.

HA HA HA HA HA HA HA HA HA HA

HA HA HA HA HA

Why is Dracula angry when he gets
out of his coffin?

He flipped his lid.

Why do vampires like the longest day of the year?

They get to sleep in.

How do we know George Washington
wasn't a vampire?

They don't make wooden fangs.

Why did the vampires fight each other?

There was bad blood between them.

What do you call a loud vampire?

A vamplifier.

How does Dracula keep his castle cool?

Scare conditioning.

Why do vampires sleep in coffins?

Because urns are too small.

Why is Dracula easy to fool?

He's a sucker.

How did the police know the vampire was guilty?

They took a blood sample.

What do you call a group of people who love Dracula?

His fang club.

FRANKENSTEIN FUNNIES

Why is Frankenstein's monster good in a crisis?

He's level-headed.

What's the best way to lock Frankenstein's neck in place?

A dead bolt.

Why is Frankenstein's monster held together with bolts, nuts, and screws?

Because he bit his nails.

HA HA

Why didn't Frankenstein's monster worry about heart attacks?

It wasn't his heart!

Why couldn't Frankenstein's monster dance?

He had two left feet.

Why were Frankenstein's shoes such a good fit?

They came with his feet.

Why was Frankenstein's monster such a good hand model?

He could leave the hand behind.

Why is Frankenstein's monster such a good listener?

He can lend you an ear.

How does Frankenstein's monster get ahead?

At the cemetery.

Which monster has a strong backbone?

Frankenspine.

Why did Frankenstein's monster wait for his bride?

She had to put on her face.

Why didn't Dr. Frankenstein have any children?

He couldn't get the parts.

How does Dr. Frankenstein like his potatoes?

Monster mashed.

Why is Frankenstein's monster a great gardener?

He has a green thumb.

Who wants Frankenstein's monster to be president?

The Green Party.

What do you call a green monster that makes good decisions?

Frankensense.

What made Frankenstein's monster believe he was put together right?

Superstitchin'.

How did Frankenstein's monster feel when he came to life?

Shocked.

Why was Frankenstein's monster so tall?

He was a *grow*-ning boy.

Why didn't Frankenstein's monster marry his girlfriend?

He wouldn't carry a torch for her.

What do you call Frankenstein's monster's son?

A chip off the old blockhead.

What kind of music does Frankenstein's monster like?

Shock 'n' Roll.

GHOULS AND FOOLS

Why did the ghost wear makeup?

To be bootiful.

Why are ghosts such bad liars?

You can see right through them.

Why are flying ghosts so happy?

They have high spirits.

What kind of bird does a ghost keep?

A boo jay.

Why do ghosts go to libraries?

Because they like booooooks.

How do ghosts stay fit?

Exorcise.

Did you hear about the ghost who couldn't swim?

She floated.

How do you know there's a ghost in your bed?

The sheets have eyeholes.

How does a ghost stick to the floor?

Superboo.

Why don't ghosts sleep in strange towns?

They're just passing through.

What does a ghost call his missing shoe?

A lost sole.

Where do you find an educated ghost?

At sghoul.

Why does a blizzard keep ghosts at home?

No sghoul today.

Where does a ghost's family live?

In an aunted house.

What do you call a ghost that
does commercials?

A spooksperson.

LOL

What do ghosts use to search the Internet?

Boogle.

Where do ghosts upload videos?

Boo Tube.

What do ghosts call a field with a lot of
people to scare?

Their haunting grounds.

How does a short ghost sit at the table?

In a booster seat.

How does a ghost sneeze?

"Ah-ah-ah-BOO!"

HA HA HA HA HA HA HA

REAL HOWLERS

What do you call the Wolfman after he shaves?

Barewolf.

What do you see when the Wolfman changes?

His underwerewolf.

How does a werewolf ask for directions?

"Hoooowl do I get there?"

When is a werewolf sad?

Once in a blue moon.

Which dessert makes a werewolf itch?

Fleas cake.

Why did the werewolf stop?

He was on paws.

What do you call a werewolf who doesn't know she changes shape?

An unawarewolf.

HA HA HA HA HA

What do you call a shape changer on a roller coaster?

A fair wolf.

Where does a baby werewolf sleep?

In a pup tent.

Why is it good to be with a werewolf who has no patience left?

He's at the end of his rope.

What did the monster say to the immature werewolf?

"Oh, growl up!"

Knock, knock!

Who's there?

Howler.

Howler who?

Howler you tonight?

FUNNY BONES

How did the skeleton cut his finger?
On his shoulder blade.

How do you know when a skeleton is angry?
He's got a bone to pick with you.

Why was the skeleton so lonely?
She had nobody.

Why are skeletons so stupid?
They're boneheads.

Why are skeletons always afraid?
They lost their nerve.

Why do skeletons give up so easily?
They don't have the heart for it.

What do you call a skeleton who's great at opera?
A prima bone-a.

Why did the skeleton take a bath?
She was bone dry.

HA

Which monster is heavier than he looks?

A skele*ton*.

- -

What did the skeleton say to his leg bone?

"How did you get in this hip joint?"

HOCUS JOCUS

Where do you find great information on spells and potions?

Witchepedia.

- -

What's the difference between a witch and a warthog?

The witch has more warts.

- -

What do witches call their worst fight?

World Wart 2.

- -

Why does the Wicked Witch make such a bad snowman?

She keeps saying, "I'm melting! I'm melting!"

- -

HA HA HA HA HA

What does a witch say when she's covered in red bumps?

"I'm welting, I'm welting!"

What does a witch say when she's recycling scrap metal?

"I'm smelting! I'm smelting!"

Where does a witch put her groceries?

In a shopping hag.

Why was the terrible witch kicked out of school?

She couldn't spell.

What do you call a witch tied up by magic words?

Spellbound.

How does a witch sign her name?

With a Magic Marker.

How does a witch know her potion is super strong?

It curls her shoes.

HA HA

What do spellcasters call hide and seek?

A witch hunt.

How does a witch send a message?

Penta-gram.

What do witches call a disgusting spell?

Mag-*ick.*

What do you call someone who can cast a spell from either side?

A witch hitter.

Why did the witch trade her broom for a vacuum cleaner?

She wanted a sweeping change.

How do you know when a witch's ride has exploded?

It goes, "Ka-BROOM!"

Knock, knock!

Who's there?

Witchcraft.

Witchcraft who?

Witchcraft project do you like better?

Knock, knock!

> Who's there?

Dispel.

> Dispel who?

Maybe dispel will open your door.

Knock, knock!

> Who's there?

Cauldron.

> Cauldron who?

Cauldron yesterday, but he didn't answer.

MERRY MUMMIES

What do you call a mummy baking in the desert heat?

> Mummifried.

Why did people think the mummy was crazy?

> He wasn't wrapped too tight.

HA HA HA

HA HA HA HA HA

How did the mummy escape from the pyramid?

She used a skeleton key.

How does a mummy secretly sell his home?

Pyramid scheme.

Why are mummies so sad?

They went from riches to rags.

Why are mummies so thirsty?

They have cotton mouth.

Why are mummies good at keeping secrets?

They keep everything under wraps.

Why didn't the mummy brush his teeth?

He only had one tooth.

Why don't mummies let their children have children?

Because then they'd be grandmummies.

HEHE

How do you make a mummy feel shame?

"Tut, tut."

Knock, knock!
Who's there?

Isis.

Isis who?

Isis the best way to cool off a mummy.

Knock, knock!

Who's there?

Pyramid.

Pyramid who?

Pyramid the bushes to find me.

YOU BEAST!

If *Bigfoot* is a Sasquatch, what's a Little Foot?

Sasquash.

What do you call a Bigfoot who won't stand?

Sasquat.

Why doesn't Sasquatch spread rumors?

He's a Bigfoot, not a Big Mouth.

How is Bigfoot like a forgotten web page?

They're both missing links.

What do you call a Bigfoot that counts trees?

A tree totaler.

How do you know when Bigfoot is in your closet?

You can see his toes under the door.

What do you call a Bigfoot who can't tell the truth?

A Big Heel.

What saying never works on Bigfoot?

"If the shoe fits, wear it."

Why did the monster charge money to cross the river?

Because it was a *troll* bridge.

What monster can't live without the Internet?

Trolls.

How did the billy goats describe the troll under the bridge?

"Baaaaaaad."

Is the Abominable Snowman ready to live with people?

Not Yeti isn't.

HA

Why do the other monsters like the
Abominable Snowman?

He's cool.

What do you call a Yeti rolling down a mountain?

An abominable snowball.

What do you call a Yeti on sale?

An affordable snowman.

Why do Yetis like blizzards?

The snow must go on.

What did the Yeti win in the beauty contest?

Best in Snow.

What does the Abominable Snowman
eat for dinner?

Spag-Yeti.

Why does the Abominable Snowman have
such big teeth?

To give you frost bite.

Why is the Abominable Snowman rude?

He gives you the cold shoulder.

Why don't you see Yetis in the classroom?

They're too cool for school.

- -

When does a Yeti land on her feet?

After a snowfall.

- -

What does a Yeti do after climbing the Himalayas?

Ever rest.

- -

Why does a Yeti go to a casino in the Himalayas?

Tibet.

- -

What's the one thing a Yeti can catch that she'll always give away?

A cold.

- -

Knock, knock!

Who's there?

Yeti.

Yeti who?

He knows who I am, Yeti still won't open the door.

- -

HA HA HA HA HA HA

LEGENDARY BEASTS

What do you call a short monster with snakes for hair?

Redusa.

Why can't you believe stories about the Minotaur?

They're half bull.

Which monster makes a great vacation guide?

A Minitour.

What kind of plates does Medusa buy?

Stoneware.

Why can't Medusa hear her victims?

She's stone deaf.

Why can't you trust Medusa in a field?

She's a snake in the grass.

What do you call a cyclops in a deck of cards?

A one-eyed jack.

HA HA HA HA HA HA HA HA

What do you call an unhappy, one-eyed monster?

Sigh-clops.

How does a scared cyclops sleep?

With one eye open.

Why are cyclops lousy pirates?

They never say, "Aye, aye."

What do you call a one-eyed hacker?

Cyberclops.

Why does Cerberus have such a big grave?

He needs three headstones.

What's the best game with three sticks?

Fetch with Cerberus.

How do you call Cerberus?

"Here, boy, boy, boy!"

Knock, knock!

Who's there?

Centaur.

Centaur who?

We Centaur best to you this holiday.

Knock, knock!

Who's there?

Hades.

Hades who?

Hades jokes are funny!

BOOK BEASTS

Which monster is not afraid of his own shadow?

The Invisible Man.

Why is the Invisible Man humble?

He can't show off.

How did the Invisible Man's girlfriend fall in love with him?

It was love at no sight.

How did the Invisible Man break up
with his girlfriend?

He said, "We shouldn't see
each other anymore."

What does the Invisible Man keep in his barn?

An invisi*bull.*

What do you get when you cross the Invisible Man
with a stop sign?

An accident.

What kind of makeup does the Invisible Man wear?

Cover-up.

What kind of makeup does the Phantom
of the Opera wear?

Maskara.

What do you call someone who loves graveyards?

A phan-tomb.

What do you call a monster who haunts a store?

Phantom of the Shopera.

HA HA HA HA HA HA

How did the Hunchback get stuck in
the church tower?

Belcro.

What's the worst gift for the Headless Horseman?

A hat.

Which monster sleeps on the floor?

The Bedless Horseman.

Why doesn't the Headless Horseman carry cash?

He always charges.

Why is a bad attack by the Headless Horseman like
a run-down battery?

He has to recharge.

What kind of horse does the Headless
Horseman ride?

A night mare.

Why doesn't the Headless Horseman
cross the road?

He can't look both ways.

Why doesn't the Headless Horseman ride through cemeteries?

Because he'd *stirrup* the dead.

What does the Headless Horseman say to his barber?

"Nothing off the top."

Monster Books

The Zombie Diet by Etta Brain

How to Make Money Like a Vampire by Rich Bloodworth

Fighting Dragons Like a Knight by Helmut On

Frankenstein's Family by Rob Graves

Lie Like the Devil by Conner Tist

Demon Possession by B. Deviled

Why the Devil Can't Fly by Angel Wing

Always Hungry by Ima Goblin

Will that Zombie Catch You? by Betty Wont

PUTTING THE DIE IN DIET

Why can't monsters go on the caveman diet?

There are no cavemen to eat anymore.

How does a vampire make hot tea?

She gets so angry her blood boils.

What's a monster's favorite tea?

Ghoul-ong.

What do zombies consider a fancy food?

Lady fingers.

What's the Abominable
Snowman's favorite food?

Cold cuts.

HEHE

How do monsters like
their chicken?

Horri-fried.

What do monsters consider fast food?

A waiter who runs away.

Why did the monster chase the garbage truck?

He was trying to catch his breakfast.

What did the monster say when she visited the junkyard?

"Wow! An all-you-can-eat buffet!"

Why do zombies like buffets?

Because two heads are better than one.

Why do monsters like it when people put out their trash?

They get to eat at the neighbor's house.

Why are monsters happy when people sunbathe?

They like a hot lunch.

Why does a sea serpent eat ships for breakfast?

It's boatmeal.

What's a monster's favorite breakfast food?

Butter on ghost.

How did the zombie lose her lunch in the shower?

Brain drain.

HA HA HA

HA HA HA HA HA

What do you call a hungry zombie?

A no-brainer.

How does a zombie feel after he loses his lunch?

Brainless.

What do you say to a zombie who hasn't eaten her first meal yet?

"Never mind."

What do zombies call a skull attached to a spine?

Brain on a stick.

Why did the zombie cry after eating someone?

His heart was in his throat.

When do you find Dracula at a blood drive?

At lunch time.

Why don't vampires eat taffy?

Their fangs stick together.

Why do vampires have a moonlight dinner?

Because they'd burn up at a sunlight breakfast.

What does a vampire call a giraffe?

A full meal.

What kind of review does a vampire give
bad-tasting blood?

Oh, negative.

What does a vampire call a straw at a blood bank?

A feeding tube.

What's Dracula's favorite dessert?

Blood pudding.

What do vampires eat with their eggs?

Blood sausage.

How does a vampire never eat eggs?

Sunny side up.

Why does Satan keep
chickens?

For deviled eggs.

What do monsters
bake at home?

Troll House
Cookies.

What does a werewolf have for dessert?

Full Moon Pies.

What's a Yeti's favorite part of the cake?

The frosting.

Why doesn't a monster wash dishes?

He eats them, too.

What's the first thing you do after a monster eats out of your hand?

Count your fingers.

What do your friends call you if a monster eats out of your right hand?

Lefty.

Why did the knight wake up the fire-breathing dragon?

He wanted to cook his eggs.

Does a monster get an ice-cream headache?

No, she gets a "you scream" headache.

HA HA HA

How does Dracula toast his marshmallows?

Over a vampfire.

What do you call a vampire who sucks the blood of pigs?

A hampire.

How do you keep Dracula out of an Italian restaurant?

Order the garlic bread.

Why did the monster cross the road?

She wanted to eat the chicken.

Why do monsters eat mold?

They need their green vegetables.

BIG-SCREEN BEASTS

What do you call King Kong in a car?

Cramped.

- -

What do you call it when King Kong fights with another giant ape?

The Thrilla with Gorillas.

- -

How does King Kong catch a flight at the airport?

With his hands.

- -

What do you call planes attacking King Kong from two sides?

Monkey in the middle.

- -

Why is King Kong a fast reader?

He can do ten stories at a time.

- -

What do you call a fire-breathing dragon who won't destroy a city?

Wreck-less.

- -

HA HA HA HA HA HA HA HA
HA HA HA HA HA HA HA HA

Why do dragons set cars on fire?

They like Hot Wheels.

What's a dragon's favorite move in a car?

A burnout.

Which monster can't keep a stiff upper lip?

The blob.

What does the blob like on its sandwiches?

Peanut blubber.

What do you get when you give the blob a bath?

A tub of goo.

Why is it so hard to make the blob angry?

It never gets bent out of shape.

Why can't the blob win an argument?

It doesn't have a leg to stand on.

Knock, knock!

Who's there?

Congo.

Congo who?

Congo up the Empire
State Building.

MORE MOVIE MONSTERS

Did you hear about the Invisible Man movie?
No one saw it.

- -

Why can't Frankenstein's monster watch
sad movies?
He falls to pieces.

- -

Why doesn't Frankenstein's monster watch
funny movies?
Because he'd laugh his head off.

- -

What kind of movie roles does the son of
Frankenstein's monster get?
Bit parts.

- -

What do actors eat when making a mummy movie?
Wraps.

- -

What did the zombies call their first action film
with plenty of chase scenes?
The Slow and the Stupid.

- - - - - - - - - - - - - - - -

HA HA

Horror Film Headlines

Werewolf Comedy a Real Howler

Nuclear Monster Movie Gets Glowing Review

Ghost Movie Lifts Your Spirit

Zombie Movie Dead at Box Office

Alien Space Movie Lands the Biggest Stars

Plot of New Mummy
Movie Unravels

Study Says
People Eat More
Popcorn During
Goblin Movies

Critics Say
Gnome More to
Underground
Movie

HA
HA
HA
HA

STAGE FRIGHT

Which monster likes to play practical jokes?
Prankenstein.

- -

Why is Frankenstein's monster
such a good comedian?
He's a real stitch.

- -

Why was Dr. Frankenstein so funny while making
his monster?
He was a real cut-up.

- -

Why are zombies such terrific comedians?
They're good at pulling your leg.

- -

Why does a zombie make fun of your mind?
She's a brain teaser.

- -

How do you make skeletons laugh?
With rib-ticklers.

- -

Why are skeletons easy to insult?
They can take a good ribbing.

How does a zombie crack a joke without smiling?

Deadpan.

Why do zombie musicians make bad dads?

They're deadbeats.

Why are zombies lousy storytellers?

Dead men tell no tales.

How do monsters with beautiful voices sing?

In *horror*mony.

What happened when the singer asked the monsters for applause?

Frankenstein's monster gave her a hand.

What did the mummies call their rock band?

The Rolling Moans.

What did the vampires call their rock band?

The Grateful Undead.

When does the Phantom of the Opera strike a chord on the piano?

When it strikes him first.

Why did the police arrest the Phantom of the Opera?

He took a bow.

Why does the Phantom of the Opera burst into song?

Because if he burst out of your chest, he'd be an alien.

Why can't gravediggers write a good story?

Too many plot holes.

Which award do you give a monster with a chest cold?

A Phlegmy.

Which TV network makes a young monster happy?

The Cartomb Network.

How can you tell when a monster is funny?

He tells a killer joke.

TINY TERRORS

Why don't leprechauns watch smart movies?

They go over their heads.

What do you get when you cross a rotting zombie with a tiny green monster?

A leper-chaun.

What do you call goblins in a fight?

Gob smacked.

Where can you dig up ghosts and goblins?

A ghoul mine.

What do you call a tiny, furry monster you find in your pocket?

Gremlint.

What is a gremlin's favorite flavor?

Grem-de-mint.

Which monster takes the train?

A choo-choocabra.

What do you call a monster that can't decide
what to eat?

A choosey-cabra.

What do you say when a chupacabra attacks a
two-headed goat?

Too baaaaaaad.

Why are chupacabras annoying?

They get your goat.

Why did the chupacabra visit the new neighbors?

They had the new kid in town.

What does a monster say to make a
goat disappear?

"Chupa-cadabra."

What do you call a short monster on wheels?

A mobile gnome.

What does a monster say when it reaches its
underground house?

There's no place like gnome.

What do you call a spirit that lives under a city?

A metro gnome.

WATER THESE MONSTERS DOING?

What do you call a serpent that doesn't clean up its room?

Loch Mess.

What do you call a water monster in jail?

Locked Ness.

How does the Loch Ness Monster get out of a cage?

She hires a Loch Smith Monster.

What do you get when you cross the Loch Ness Monster with a candy bar?

Nessie Milk Chocolate.

Where does Nessie keep her books?

In her Loch-er.

HA HA HA HA HA
HA HA HA HA HA HA HA HA
HA HA HA HA HA HA

Where does a flying lake monster live?

Loch Nest.

How did the sea serpent feel when she found the sunken ship?

She was a wreck.

How do you know when a sea serpent is angry?

He has a hissy fit.

How does a sea serpent find its way in the ocean?

With a GPSssssssss.

What do you call a lake with no monsters?

Empty Ness.

What do you call a lake monster with no friends?

Lonely Ness.

What do you call it when Nessie can't speak?

Loch jaw.

How does a sea monster find out whether or not a boat fits her head?

She capsizes it.

How do you cheer up a sea serpent?

With a clown fish.

What do you call a swamp monster doing spring cleaning?

A muckraker.

Why was the monster chillin' in a swamp?

He was getting his marsh mellow on.

How does a swamp monster like his sandwich?

Full of peanut butter, and smelly.

How does a swamp monster escape?

She gets bayou.

WHAT'CHA GONNA CALL?

What do you call a vampire who's never wrong?
Exactula.

What do you call a skeleton learning the alphabet?
T-bone.

What do you call a vampire at noon?
Ash.

What do you call a monster in the woods?
Hunter.

What do you call a monster with a long, furry coat?
Harry.

What do you call a monster who catches you
to win the race?
Victor.

HAHA

What do you call a sea monster who can't swim?

Bob.

What do you call a monster who steals?

Robin.

What do you call a monster who can't tell the truth?

Liza.

What do you call a vampire who robs banks?

Vaulter.

What do you call a zombie who won't stop talking?

Mona.

What do you call a friendly ghost bear?

Winnie the Boo.

What do you call a giant, stupid ape?

Ding Dong.

What do you call an ill sea monster?

Moby Sick.

What do you call a witch at the gym?

Miss Fit.

What do you call a monster who skips school?

The Hooky Monster.

What do you call a new monster?

The Rookie Monster.

What do you call a team of Yeti superheroes?

The Just Ice League.

What do you call a team of vampire superheroes?

The Fangtastic Four.

HA
HA
HA

Monster Facts

Did you know that if you give a monster a penny for his thoughts you get money back?

Did you know that you can lead a monster to water, but you can't bathe away the stink?

Did you know that if you charge Frankenstein's monster an arm and a leg, he'll pay it?

Did you know that there's nothing a zombie won't be caught dead doing?

Did you know that a ghoul and his money are soon parted?

Did you know that at the end of every rainbow is a monster stealing a pot of gold?

Did you know that you should never trust a zombie that says, "Let me pick your brain"?

Did you know that when a monster bites the bullet, he goes back for a second bullet?

MAD, MAD WORLD

Where did the mad scientist keep his dead lab rodents?

In a mouse-eleum.

What kind of dog does a mad scientist have?

A laboratory retriever.

Why did the mad scientist bring dried grapes to the graveyard?

She was raisin the dead.

Why did the mad scientist send his monster to the auction?

To do his bidding.

Where does a mad scientist live?

In a madhouse.

Why was Dr. Frankenstein digging in the sand?

He wanted to give his monster a beach body.

HA HA HA HA HA HA

What kind of flowers did Dr. Frankenstein give his monster?

Two-lips.

How did Dr. Frankenstein make his monster clumsy?

He gave him all thumbs.

What did Dr. Frankenstein say when he put the last bolt in his monster?

"That was a pain in the neck!"

How did Dr. Frankenstein's mom protect him during his electrical experiment?

She grounded him.

Knock, knock!

Who's there?

Masterful.

Masterful who?

Masterful, Igor hungry.

THE BEST MONSTER FOR THE JOB

When is a zombie a florist?

When she's pushing up daisies.

- -

What does a zombie grow in his vegetable garden?

Whatever it is, he won't eat it.

- -

What does a vampire grow on his farm?

Blood oranges.

- -

What's Dracula's job at NASA?

The *Count*down.

- -

How do you pay a vampire?

In blood money.

- -

How do you pay a Yeti?

In cold cash.

- -

When do you pay a monster more to scare people?

When he's working ogre time.

How do you pay Frankenstein's monster?

In greenbacks.

Why do grave robbers make good reporters?

They can dig up a story.

Why do evil spirits make terrific salespeople?

They give a great demon-stration.

What do you call a monster who stays home to raise a child?

The primary scaregiver.

How did Quasimodo solve the murder?

He followed his hunch.

What do you call Quasimodo jumping in a hotel?

A bell hop.

Which monster always has a lot of work?

The swamped monster.

What do you call a zombie with a lot of money?

Filthy rich.

TENDER LOVING SCARE

What do you call a vampire with a fever?

Hot-blooded.

How long does a monster stink?

About a reek.

What score did the eye doctor give the hundred-eyed monster on his eye test?

20/20/20/20/20/20 . . .

How do monsters treat you at the hospital?

With good healthscare.

HA HA HA HA HA

How do you make a body disappear at the morgue?

Abracadaver.

How did the zombie get through med school?

As a corpse.

When does a monster use dental floss?

When someone is stuck in his teeth.

What do you call a vampire with asthma?

Vlad the Inhaler.

What did the dentist say to the vampire?

"Fang loose, I'll be right back."

Why did the monster put his eye back in?

To get a second look.

What do you call a short, limping monster?

A hobblin' goblin.

HA HA HA
HA HA
HA HA HA

WHAT A DRAG

Why do dragons sleep during the day?

They fight knights.

Which knight sneaks up on dragons?

Sir Prise.

What do you call a knight who cuts a dragon with a scalpel?

Sir Jen.

What do you call a knight who draws weird pictures of dragons?

Sir Real.

What do you call a knight who won't take his eyes off a dragon?

Sir Glancelot.

What did the dragons give a sleeping Sir Lancelot?

Knight terrors.

How do you hide from a dragon in the dark?

Turn out the knight light.

Which flower does a knight hunt?

Snapdragons.

Did you hear about the dragon
party on the farm?

It was a real barn burner.

Knock, knock!

Who's there?

Demote.

Demote who?

Demote won't stop de dragon.

HA
HA

WHAT DO YOU CALL THAT THING?

What do you get when you cross Frankenstein's monster with a candle?

A wax dummy.

- -

What do you get when you cross Bigfoot with a skunk?

A big stink.

- -

What do you get when you cross Sasquatch with a mushroom?

A Bigfoot Fungus.

- -

What do you get when you cross a vampire with Bigfoot?

A bat whose feet are too heavy to fly.

- -

What do you get when you cross a vampire with a giant lollipop?

An all-day bloodsucker.

What do you get when you cross a vampire
with a bell?

A dingbat.

What do you get when you cross an unblinking
monster with a floating rock?

A stareroid.

What do you get when you cross a mummy
with a hippo?

A mummy with a tummy.

What do you get when you cross the Minotaur
with a train?

A bull ride.

What do you get when you cross a blood-sucking
monster with a snake?

A chupa-cobra.

What do you get when you cross an evil spirit
with a chicken?

Poultrygeist.

HEHE

What do you get when you cross Dracula
with a phoenix?

A vampire who can rise from the ashes.

What do you get when you cross Dracula
with Frankenstein?

Fangenstein.

What do you get when you cross a zombie
with the Hunchback of Notre Dame?

A dead ringer.

What do you get when you cross a Yeti with a
horrible singer?

An abominable showman.

What do you get when you cross the Wolfman
with Superman?

A werewolf that changes in a phone booth.

What do you get when you cross the Abominable
Snowman with a leprechaun?

Wintergreen.

What do you get when you cross a wizard with a
four-leaf clover?

A warluck.

What do you get when you cross a Yeti with a fire-breathing dragon?

Freezer burn.

What do you get when you cross a mad scientist with an ogre?

A genius whose ideas stink.

What do you get when you cross a monster with a skunk?

A better-smelling monster.

HOLIDAY SPIRITS

Why does Santa Claus visit Bigfoot in June?

It takes six months to fill his stocking.

What kind of trees do monsters decorate at Christmas?

Frankenpine.

HA HA HA HA
HA HA HA HA

What do you call a werewolf at Christmas?
Santa Claws.

What do you call happy Christmas ghosts?
Holiday spirits.

How does a werewolf wish you happy holidays?
"Happy Hoooooowlidays!"

Why do ghosts love the Fourth of July?
Because their favorite colors are red, white, and boo.

How do monsters trick-or-treat in cemeteries?
In costombs.

Which monster likes Thanksgiving?
A gobble-in.

HA HA

What's a vampire's favorite holiday?

Fangsgiving.

Knock, knock!

Who's there?

Handsome.

Handsome who?

Handsome of that Halloween candy to me.

DEADBALL!

What do you call Frankenstein's monster in a boxing ring?

A punching dummy.

Why did the zombie attack the boxer?

She wanted a knuckle sandwich.

Why did the boxer tie up Frankenstein's monster?

He wanted to rope-a-dope.

Why do monsters go to football games?

To eat whoever makes the catch of the day.

HA HA HA HA HA HA HA HA HA HA
HA HA HA HA HA HA HA HA HA HA

Why is Frankenstein's monster such a good running back?

He stiff-arms the defense.

Why don't villagers near Frankenstein's castle play baseball?

Because they pitch forks.

When do you play with Dracula and Cinderella?

When you need a bat and a ball.

How do you capture a baseball-loving vampire?

In a *bat*-ting cage.

Which monster is a great basketball player?

The hoopacabra.

HA HA HA HA

Why did the monster punch the soccer field?

He wanted to hit the pitch.

What did Nessie say when asked if she'd win the race?

"It's a Loch."

How did the zombie do in the race?

He finished dead last.

How did the vampire do in the race?

She finished undead last.

Did you hear about the spirit who ran marathons?

She ghosts the distance.

What was wrong with the skeleton's deck of cards?

No hearts.

What was wrong with the gravedigger's deck of cards?

All spades.

Why doesn't the Abominable Snowman work out?

Because then he'd be the Abdominal Snowman.

What do monsters call their car-racing league?

NASCARE.

Do zombies arm wrestle?

No, the arms can wrestle on their own.

Why are voodoo dolls lousy wrestlers?

They get pinned.

SCARE TACTICS

Which monster joined the army?

Tankenstein.

Which army officer did Dracula bite?

Major Pain in the Neck.

What do monster sergeants give out?

Corporal punishment.

HA HA HA HA
HA HA HA HA

What do you call a ghost in the army?

Boo-tenant.

Where do you put vampires in the army?

In a bat-talion.

How does an army of monsters win a war?

Scare tactics.

Why didn't Bigfoot's mother wear combat boots?

They were too small.

Where do ugly monsters live?

Monstross City.

Which city has the
fewest people to scare?

Scare City.

What's a ghost's favorite
city?

Boo-ston.

Where do monsters in Missouri live?

St. Pewie.

Where can you find two-headed monsters
in France?

Pair-us.

Which German city has snow monsters?

Burrr-lin.

HA HA HA HA HA HA HA HA

Which Canadian city has the most vampires?

Fangcouver.

What do you call a monster in Brooklyn?

Scared.

What do you get when you put werewolves at the North Pole?

An ice pack.

What does a monster put on at the beach?

Sunscream.

How do monsters keep out of the sun in France?

They hide in the chateaus.

How does a ghost scare animals in Australia?

"Kangaboo!"

HA HA HA HA
HA HA
HA HA HA HA
HA HA HA HA

BFFS
(BEST FIENDS FOREVER)

What's the difference between Frankenstein's monster and the Wolfman?

One clobbers, and the other slobbers.

Why didn't Dracula trust the Wolfman?

Werewolves are two-faced.

What did Frankenstein's monster say when he met Dracula?

"'Pire bad!"

Why did Frankenstein's monster give Dracula a goose-feather pillow?

It was down for the Count.

How did the ghost and the skeleton die?

Boo-bone-ic plague.

How did the skeleton describe meeting the Abominable Snowman?

Spine-chilling.

Why did Cinderella date a Yeti?

To go to the Snow Ball.

What is the difference between a zombie and someone with a sunburn?

A zombie's skin already peeled off.

MONSTER MANIA

Why did the monster spin its head all the way around?

To talk back.

How does an old woman turn herself into an angry green monster?

Gramma rays.

Did you hear about the monster who bragged too much?

He went ogre the top.

What do monsters say when they clink their glasses together?

"Fears!"

Where do uncles meet their dead wives?

Se-aunts.

On what day are witches chased out of town?

Shunday.

On what day do werewolves howl at the sky?

Moonday.

What's the best day for a monster to scare you?

Terri-Friday.

Why does a monster drink coffee?

For the caffiend.

Why did the monster turn on the air conditioner?

To keep ghoul.

How does a monster win a popularity contest?

By being the ghoulest.

What do you call a monster in the second grade?

Brilliant.

Why can't monsters spell?

"Roar!" isn't a letter.

Why do monsters use onions to play
number games?

Because they stink at math.

- -

Why is the principal afraid of the monster?

It cut school.

- -

What do you call a rotten monster who thinks
he owns everything?

Spoiled.

- -

How do the dead communicate?

Zomb-e-mail.

- -

How do monsters ship packages
by train?

In a fright car.

- -

What do you call someone who goes to graveyards to get rich?

A ghoul digger.

Do you think the Bogeyman is nice?

He's snot.

What kind of pet does a monster keep in a bowl?

A ghoulfish.

Which monster doesn't like joke books?

The Grim Reader.

What do you call a scary ringtone?

A Grim Beeper.

What do you call a serious monster that sneaks up on you?

The Grim Creeper.

What kind of trouble does a two-headed monster get into?

Double Trouble.

What happens when half of a two-headed monster dies?

It departs.

What do you call a two-headed monster in a winter coat?

A two-fur.

What present do you give a slobbering monster?

Droolery.

How many monsters does it take to change a lightbulb?

None. They like the dark.

What type of monster never leaves a hotel?

A polterguest.

What do monsters call a pajama party?

A creepover.

HEHE

How do you know when a monster is under your bed?

The dust bunnies are scared.

Why do monsters hide in your closet?

Because your sock drawer is too small.

How do you know when a monster has been in your closet?

Your shirts are stretched out.

How do you know when there's a monster under your bed?

The snoring keeps you awake.

How do you know when monsters are in your closet?

They hanger-round.

Why did the scared monster think someone was at the door?

His knees were knocking.

How did the monster stop the scarecrow?

She beat the stuffing out of him.

Why did the monster stab his clock?

To kill time.

What does a monster say after it claws you to death?

"Rest in pieces."

HA HA HA HA HA

How do you know when a monster is lazy?

He doesn't even chew his person.

How does a monster strangle you quickly?

Full throttle.

How do you keep a monster with 1,000 hands from going crazy?

Tell him to get a grip.

What do you call the slipperiest, gooiest monster ever?

The greatest of all-slime.

Who do monsters call when they need adult supervision?

Their mummy.

What's the best kind of party to give a monster?

A going-away party.

What kind of party do the lice on Frankenstein's head have?

A block party.

Why did the monster like to scare girls?

He was a real go-get-her.

How did the monster get hurt at the barber shop?

He brought a chainsaw for his buzzcut.

How do you know when a monster has a girlfriend?

He starts bathing twice a year.

How does a monster get shiny hair?

Scare conditioner.

What do monsters like about shampoo?

The poo.

What two words scare a monster away?

Bath time.

Why did the monster hide in the bathtub?

It was the last place anyone would look.

HA HA HA HA
HA HA HA HA HA
HA HA HA HA
HA HA HA HA HA

DO YOU HEAR A KNOCKING?

Knock, knock!

> Who's there?

Uno.

> Uno who?

Uno there's a monster out here, right?

- -

Knock, knock!

> Who's there?

Funnel.

> Funnel who?

Funnel start when the monsters get here.

- -

Knock, knock!

> Who's there?

Voodoo.

> Voodoo who?

Voodoo you think it is?

- -

HA HA HA HA

Knock, knock!

> Who's there?

Donut.

> Donut who?

Donut open the door if it's a monster.

Knock, knock!

> Who's there?

Demonize.

> Demonize who?

Demonize can steal your soul.

Knock, knock!

> Who's there?

Devilish.

> Devilish who?

The Devilish shtanding outshide your door.

HA HA HA

Knock, knock!

Who's there?

Closet.

Closet who?

Run if a monster closet this door.

Knock, knock!

Who's there?

Darren.

Darren who?

Darren a monster to fight is stupid.

Knock, knock!

Who's there?

Etta.

Etta who?

That monster Etta lot.

Knock, knock!

Who's there?

Wooden stakes.

Wooden stakes who?

Wooden stakes be a great way to kill a vampire?

- -

Knock, knock!

Who's there?

Despair.

Despair who?

Despair doesn't taste good.

- -

Knock, knock!

Who's there?

Venom.

Venom who?

Venom out here, vould you let me in?

- -

Knock, knock!

Who's there?

Roman.

Roman who?

Roman around a haunted house is stupid.

- -

HA HA HA HA

Knock, knock!
Who's there?
Bitter.
Bitter who?
Dracula bitter on the neck.

Knock, knock!
Who's there?
Frighten.
Frighten who?
Frighten burgers because I brought a lot of friends.

Knock, knock!
Who's there?
Villainy.
Villainy who?
Villainy one let me in?

Knock, knock!
Who's there?
Afraid.
Afraid who?
Afraid knot won't hold Frankenstein.

Knock, knock!
 Who's there?
Isabel.
 Isabel who?
Isabel enough to wake up a monster?

Knock, knock!
 Who's there?
Uno.
 Uno who?
Uno there's still a monster out here, right?

ABOUT THE AUTHOR

John Briggs is a veteran comedy writer whose jokes have appeared on TV, radio, and in print. In addition to performing thousands of shows across the country, he once served as the opening act for HBO's *Young Young Comedians* talent search. He's the author of the picture book *Leaping Lemmings!* and *Just for Kicks!* (both Sterling) and lives in upstate NY.

Find out more about him at johnbriggsbooks.net.